GEOGRAPHY *for fun*

People and Places

Pam Robson

Copper Beech Books
Brookfield, Connecticut

Produced by
Aladdin Books Ltd
28 Percy Street
London W1P 0LD

First published in the United States
in 2001 by
Copper Beech Books,
an imprint of
The Millbrook Press
2 Old New Milford Road
Brookfield, Connecticut 06804

Editor: Kathy Gemmell

Designer: Simon Morse

Illustrator: Tony Kenyon

Picture researcher: Brian Hunter Smart

Printed in UAE

Library of Congress Cataloging-in-Publication Data

Robson, Pam.
People and places / Pam Robson ; [illustrator, Tony Kenyon.]
p.cm. -- (Geography for fun)
Includes index.
ISBN 0-7613-2423-2 (lib. bdg.)
1. Geography--Juvenile Literature. [1. Geography. 2. Geographical
recreations.] I. Kenyon, Tony, ill. II. Title.
G133. R62 2001
910--dc21

2001028820

The author, Pam Robson, is an experienced teacher.
she has written and advised on many books for
children on geography and science subjects.

CONTENTS

INTRODUCTION

Geography is about people and places and all the changes that take place in the world. How the shape of the land changes over time. How people change their surroundings when they chop down forests and build roads and houses. How people manufacture goods using natural materials. Geography is about all these things. You will discover how people change the world, why these changes happen, and what the consequences are for our planet.

1 Look for numbers like this. Each step for the projects inside the book has been numbered this way. To draw the maps, make the games, and complete the projects, make sure you follow the steps in the right order.

FEATURE BOXES
● Look for the feature boxes on each double page. They either give more information about the project on the page, or they suggest other interesting activities for you to do.

HELPFUL HINTS

- Look for Helpful Hints on some pages—they give you tips for doing the projects.

- Look at the Glossary at the back of this book to find out what important words mean.

- Always use up-to-date maps, atlases, websites, and reference books.

WARNING

- This sign means that you must be careful. Ask an adult to help you when you use a sharp cutting tool or electrical appliance. Always tell an adult where you are going and what you are doing when you collect information for the projects.

SETTLEMENTS

A settlement is a place where people live. It can be very small, with only a few houses, or as large as a city, where millions of people live. A city has lots of stores and offices and provides services, such as hospitals and schools, for its people. A long time ago, people built settlements close to rivers, because they provided water and were the best way to transport goods. New Orleans grew up at a good location on the Mississippi River.

Street map

x My house

Continent map

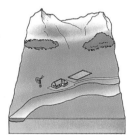

A house is built by a river for water and easy transportation.

Roads are built and a town forms as more people settle.

The town expands into a city, with services, factories, and many roads.

WHERE YOU LIVE

Make a "nest" of four maps, each on a different scale, to show the first four lines of your address.

1 Use a large-scale map to find the street you live on.

Paola Zaghini
14 Appian Way
Rome
Italy
Europe
The Northern Hemisphere
The World
The Galaxy
The U

2 Find the location of your village, town, or city in an atlas. Is there a river nearby? Now find your country. What shape is it? Does it have a coastline? Find the name of the continent in which you live.

Town location map

Country map

3 Now draw four maps, as shown. Make sure you put in natural features, like rivers. Glue the maps onto cardboard and label them.

HELPFUL HINTS

● The scale on each map is different. A street map is large scale; a continent map is small scale. To get the scale right, trace from the atlas.

● Practice using scale by doing map "nests" for places you hear about in the news.

TYPES OF SETTLEMENT

● The area around a settlement is its location. A village is a rural location, which means it is surrounded by countryside. A town or city is an urban location—a built-up area, with many buildings and services.

CITY
Large urban location. Services include stores, offices, factories, places of worship, schools, hospitals, museums, theaters, restaurants, post offices, galleries, roads, and public transportation.

TOWN
Smaller than a city, but with similar services (in big towns). Small towns usually have one main shopping area.

VILLAGE
Up to 2,000 people. Services may include stores, a post office, a school, and public transportation.

HAMLET
Fewer than 50 people. Few services.

FARM or HOMESTEAD
One family. No services, except for electricity and telephone (in developed countries).

● Settlements built on the outskirts of cities are called suburbs. Suburbs sometimes stretch to join up with towns or villages nearby. Together, a city and its suburbs make a metropolitan area.

SHORT JOURNEYS

People make journeys every day. Each time you leave your house—to go school, to a friend's house, or to the store—you are making a journey. There are different ways to travel a short distance—on foot or by bicycle, car, train, or bus. It usually takes longer to walk, but it is good exercise. People drive to supermarkets to shop. Parents often drive their children to school. Many people commute (travel to work each day) by car, bus, or train.

JOURNEY TIMES

Carry out a survey with a group of friends to find out how you all travel to school. Present your information on a chart. You will need cardboard, scissors, paper, glue, and colored pencils.

Brian
3 mi
20 mins

Tony
2 mi
15 mins

Lisa
2 1/2 mi
20 mins

Tasmin
1/4 mi
5 mins

Jin Soo
1 1/2 mi
15 mins

1 First, write out a list of questions to ask. Do you travel to school by car, bus, or train? Do you walk or bicycle? How far from school do you live? How long does your journey take? Record all of your friends' answers on a sheet of paper.

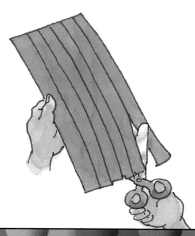

2 Cut out a strip of colored cardboard for each friend. Cut one end of each cardboard strip into an arrow shape.

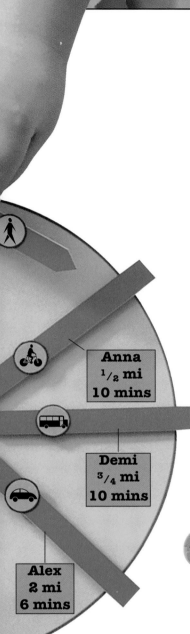

Anna
$^1/_2$ mi
10 mins

Demi
$^3/_4$ mi
10 mins

Alex
2 mi
6 mins

PEDESTRIANS

● People who walk along sidewalks and footpaths are called pedestrians. In Britain, some children walk to school in a "walking bus." Parents lead the "bus" and collect children along the route.

● Children in some parts of the world have to walk many miles each day to get to school.

3 Draw a symbol of your school in the center of a large cardboard circle. Arrange the arrows around the school. Draw transportation symbols, as shown here. Glue the correct symbol onto each arrow. Write labels on small slips of paper to show how far each person travels and how long it takes.

 Car

 Bus

Bicycle

Walk

4 Now rearrange the arrows to show how each person travels home from school. Do they use the same forms of transportation as they used in the morning? Make new arrows, symbols, and labels for any changes.

SERVICES CHART

● Redo the chart to show the services you visit from home, such as stores and the library. Put your home at the center of the circle and arrange the arrows to show which form of transportation you use to get to each service. Write labels to show distances and journey times.

LONG JOURNEYS

In earlier times, large numbers of people moved from one region to another, seeking better living conditions and opportunities. But traveling was hard, and people moved short distances. Today, we live in a global community, in which many people can travel long distances quickly and easily. The result is that people from many different countries now live in cities like New York or London, yet keep their ties to family members in their countries of origin.

A MOVING STORY

Make a "family map" to show all the places that you and your family have links with. You need a large map of the world, a pencil, tracing paper, colored yarn, scissors, and pushpins.

Grandparents' generation (2 twists)

1 Do some research about your family tree. Ask questions and look in family albums. Where were you born? Where were your parents and grandparents born? If you have a stepfamily, include them in your research too.

2 Trace the part of the world map you need. It may be just one country if your family has always lived there. Color it and label the continents, countries, or towns. Mark your birthplace in pencil. Draw an arrow from there to the place you lived next, then to the place after that, and so on.

3 Cut lengths of yarn. Choose a different color for each generation of your family. Pin one end of your color of yarn to the place where you were born. Follow the arrows with the yarn, pinning it at each new place.

Parents' generation (1 twist)

4 To show the "life journey" taken by your parents and grandparents, twist different colors of yarn around your first strand. Add a twist for each generation. Place and pin the twists as you did for your own life journey. Write labels to show the dates your family moved from place to place.

MIGRATION

● People move for many different reasons, both within their own country and to other countries. Some move to live near family members who have already migrated.

● Some families move from the countryside to large cities to look for work. Most people in developed countries now live in urban locations.

● Some people escape the pollution and litter of cities to live in the countryside. Sometimes, they commute (travel every day) to work in the city.

● People who are forced to leave their own country, because they are living in danger, are called refugees. They seek refuge (a place to feel safe) in other countries. There are many thousands of refugees in the world today. Some escape from war or cruelty, and others flee from natural disasters, such as earthquakes or floods.

WORLD WEATHER

Climate—the usual pattern of weather in a place—affects the way people live. Climate depends mainly on latitude, which is how far north or south of the equator a place is (see below). Countries in tropical latitudes, close to the equator, have a hot, wet climate. Countries in temperate latitudes (between the tropics and the poles) have a mild climate. Altitude, which means height above sea level, also affects climate. Places at high altitudes are always cool, no matter where in the world they are.

LATITUDE AND LONGITUDE

● Numbered lines on maps and globes show latitude (horizontal lines) and longitude (vertical lines). Latitude is measured north or south of the equator, the zero degree (0°) line of latitude. The tropics lie between 0° and 23°N and 23°S. Temperate regions lie between the tropics and 60°N and 60°S. Longitude is measured in degrees east or west of the prime meridian, which runs through London, England.

Prime meridian

60°N

Temperate region

23°N

Tropics

Equator, 0°

CHART IT

Make a chart to show the climate in cities in different parts of the world. You will need an atlas, tracing paper, pencils, a ruler, scissors, and glue.

Aswan
24°N, 32°E
Aswan is in Egypt, on the bank of the Nile River. The climate is very hot and dry—it hardly ever rains there. July is the hottest month.

Bogota
4°N, 74°W

1 Look in the atlas index to find the country and continent in which each city is located. Trace country maps from the atlas and mark the location of each city you have chosen. Glue the maps onto your chart. Find the latitude and longitude for each city from the numbers on the atlas map grids.

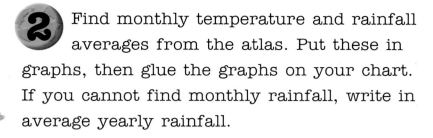

Write labels about each place. Does it get a lot of rain? Which is the hottest month?

2 Find monthly temperature and rainfall averages from the atlas. Put these in graphs, then glue the graphs on your chart. If you cannot find monthly rainfall, write in average yearly rainfall.

Temperature °F
110
90
70
50
30
10
-10

J F M A M J J A S O N D

Rainfall = virtually none

Bogotá is in Colombia. It is very high, so it never gets very hot.

Temperature °F
90
70
50
30
10
-10

Rainfall, inches
20
16
12
8
4
0

J F M A M J J A S O N D

Manila is in the Philippines in Southeast Asia. It rains a lot and is hot most of the year. The climate is very humid.

Temperature °F
90
70
50
30
10
-10

Rainfall, inches
20
16
12
8
4
0

J F M A M J J A S O N D

Manila
14°N, 121°E

Latitude and longitude

SEASONS

● Places in temperate regions have four seasons a year. Seasons happen because the Earth tilts on its axis as it circles the Sun. As one hemisphere (half of the Earth) leans toward the Sun, it has summer, while the other hemisphere leans away, and has winter. The Earth takes a full year to circle the Sun. The Sun shines almost directly over the equator all year, so it is always hot there.

Summer in the southern hemisphere

Winter in the northern hemisphere

Sun

Equator

Summer in the northern hemisphere

Winter in the southern hemisphere

● In tropical places, there are only two seasons each year, a wet season and a dry season. Floods often occur in the wet season. In rural parts of developing countries, this makes travel hard.

HOMES

Climate and location—whether a place is urban or rural—determine what kinds of home people build. In places with a cold climate, houses often have basements and double-glazed windows. In hot countries, homes must provide shade from the Sun. In areas with high rainfall, roofs must be sloped to let water run off easily. Urban locations in every climate usually have apartment houses, where many people can live in a small area.

TEMPERATE CLIMATE HOMES
Brick, stone, or wood, with big windows to let in light. Sloping roofs let rain run off easily.

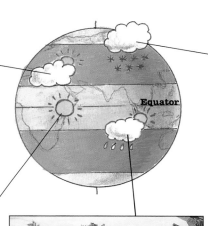

Equator

COLD CLIMATE HOMES
Sloping, ridged roofs with an overhang to protect balconies and people below from sliding snow. Often wooden walls.

HOT, DRY CLIMATE HOMES
Often rectangular, with a flat roof. Small windows and thick walls keep out the Sun.

HOT, WET CLIMATE HOMES
Often wooden walls, raised on platforms to allow cool air to circulate. Roofs often made from corrugated iron.

PLAY THE HOUSE GAME
Learn about climates and homes by making this card game for two players. You will need cardboard and colored pencils.

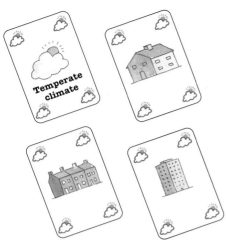

Temperate climate set
Cold climate set

1 First, copy and cut out two of each card shown here, so that you have 32 cards altogether. Each set represents one climate. Three cards show house types and one is the matching climate card.

2 Deal four cards each. Lay the remaining cards face down in a pile. The first player picks up the top card then throws a card away. Lay the unwanted cards face up in a pile. The next player can pick up the top card from either pile. The winner is the first to collect one full set.

Hot, wet climate set
Hot, dry climate set

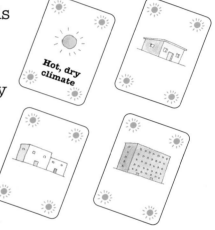

SHANTY TOWNS

● In developing countries, many very poor people live in shanty towns on the outskirts of large cities. Most have moved near the city to find work. They live in makeshift shanties built of cardboard, corrugated metal, or plywood. The shanty towns have no running water or electricity.

POLLUTING THE STREETS

Pollution in the world's many busy cities can make them unpleasant, dirty places to live in. Air pollution is caused by burning fossil fuels in homes, factories, and cars, which produces smoke and exhaust gases. Litter is also a form of pollution. Most litter that people leave behind in streets and parks is packaging, such as chip bags and drink cartons. Some litter is dangerous—broken bottles can cut people, and plastic bags can suffocate animals or small children.

CLEAN SWEEP

Learn how to dispose of the trash we find around us by making and playing the litter game. You will need cardboard, scissors, glue, and colored pencils.

1 Ask an adult to help you cut out a board from cardboard. Color it to look like a local park.

2 Cut out 20 red cards. On each, draw an item of trash that you might find in a park.

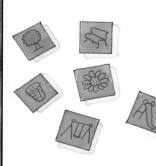

3 Cut out 20 green cards. Leave 10 cards blank. Draw pictures of objects you would like to see in the park, such as flowers and benches, onto the other 10 cards. Cut out 20 smaller cards. Put a minus sign on 10 of them and a plus sign on the other 10. Shuffle them and lay them face down in a pile.

4 Make a tray with four compartments, as shown below. Color and label each one with a different way of dealing with trash.

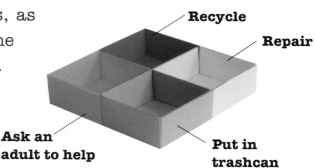

Recycle
Repair
Ask an adult to help
Put in trashcan

This is a game where you all work together, so make sure you discuss where to put the new items and what to do with the old ones.

5 The aim of the game is to work as a team to clear the park of trash. Place the 20 red litter cards over the board to look like litter on the ground. Take turns picking a card from the plus or minus card pile. If you pick a minus card, remove a piece of trash. Discuss with the team what to do with it, then put it in the correct section in the tray. Can it be recycled? Should it be thrown in the trashcan? Is it dangerous? Should you ask an adult to help?

6 If you pick a plus card, select a green card. If it has a picture on it, discuss the best place to put it in the park. If it is blank, draw what you would like to see in the park, then position it. The game finishes when there is no litter left and the park has been "landscaped."

RECYCLING
● Waste paper, glass, and aluminum cans can be recycled (processed to be used again). Glass bottles and aluminum cans can be collected, melted down, and made into new bottles and cans. Plastic bottles can also be recycled. Sort containers as directed.

A CROWDED WORLD

As population increases and more people need homes, many parts of the world are becoming overcrowded. A quarter of the world's population now lives in cities and the cities are gradually spreading into vast metropolitan areas. Some cities and countries are more crowded than others. France, for example, has the same population as Britain, but because France is bigger, it is less crowded. We say its population density is lower than Britain's. Population density is the average number of people per square kilometer (km^2) of land.

Bangladesh
847 people per km^2

Taiwan
606 people per km^2

United Kingdom
238 people per km^2

Botswana
3 people per km^2

Colombia
32 people per km^2

U.S.A.
29 people per km^2

Population density per km^2	
200+	**40-100**
100-200	**10-40**
	under 10

DENSITY BAR CHART

Make a population density bar chart. You will need a long cardboard tube, cardboard, a ruler, scissors, and paint. Use the map above or an atlas to find out population densities in the countries you want to show.

People per km^2

900+
800
700
600
500
400
300
200
100

USA

1 Choose a scale for your "bars," such as 5 cm (2 in) = 100 people per km². Measure and cut lengths of cardboard roll for each country. Paint and label each "bar."

2 Draw and label grid lines across the cardboard, starting about 20 cm (8 in) from the bottom. Fold the bottom to make a base. Glue the "bars" in place.

POPULATION GROWTH

● The population of the world has greatly increased over the last 50 years. In 1999, the United Nations declared that the world's six billionth baby had been born in Bosnia.

10 million	200 million	420 million	1.2 billion	2.5 billion	6 billion	11 billion
100,000 years ago	2,000 years ago	500 years ago	1850	1950	2000	2050 (estimated)

● As population has grown, people have cleared more and more of the world's forests. Some are cut down to harvest the wood, some to make room to grow crops, and some to provide land for building houses and roads.

6,000 years ago **2,000 years ago** **Today**

Land — Forest Forest — Land

● Population density can also be measured in people per square mile. If you know population per square kilometer, multiply that number by 2.59 to find the population per square mile.

19

RAW MATERIALS

Everything we use and everything around us is made from material of some kind. Materials that are changed or treated to be made into something else are called raw materials. One important raw material is cotton. The cotton plants need to be picked, cleaned, and processed before being made into fabric for clothes. Finished products, like cotton shirts, are called manufactured goods.

Iron ore

Limestone

Coke

Furnace

Iron

Iron ore is a mineral that is dug from the ground. It is heated in huge furnaces with coke and limestone. The iron separates as a very hot liquid and is poured into molds, where it cools and hardens.

ANIMAL, VEGETABLE, OR MINERAL?

Play this game to learn what different objects are made from. You will need small pictures of objects made from various materials, glue, and cardboard.

1 Draw or cut out pictures of objects from magazines. Glue each picture onto cardboard. Think about the raw materials used to make each one. A leather bag is made from animal hide (skin), so it is grouped as "animal." A book is made from wood pulp, so it is grouped as "vegetable." An iron railing is made from iron ore (see left), so it is classed as "mineral."

2 Write "animal," "vegetable," or "mineral" on the back of each object card. Use these pictures (right) to help you. Anything made from a plant is vegetable. Now quiz your friends. Hold up each card and ask, "Animal, vegetable, or mineral?" The player who gives the right answer keeps the card. The winner is the player with most cards.

String—vegetable (sisal or cotton)

Fork—mineral (metal)

Scarf—animal (wool)

Apple—vegetable (apple tree)

Glass—mineral (sand)

Cotton— vegetable (cotton plant)

Pencil—vegetable and mineral (wood and graphite)

Soap—animal or vegetable (animal or vegetable fat)

Plastic spoon— mineral (oil)

Leather shoes— animal (animal hide)

BRICKS

● Most bricks are made of clay and sand. These raw materials are ground together, then mixed with water and molded into  brick shapes. When the bricks have dried, they are fired in a very hot oven called a kiln to make them hard. The ancient Romans used triangular bricks, but most modern bricks are rectangular.

● To build walls, the finished bricks are laid in layers and stuck together with a cement mixture called mortar.

JOBS AND RESOURCES

People need to work to earn money to pay for food, clothing, and homes. A long time ago, most people worked on the land directly, as hunters or farmers. Then people began to work in manufacturing industries, using the Earth's natural resources—raw materials like wood—to turn into manufactured goods, such as paper. More people were then needed to work selling the manufactured goods. Today, few people work on the land in developed countries. Most work in offices and stores, or in jobs working with people, such as teaching.

PAPER-MAKING

Paper-making uses up one of the Earth's valuable natural resources —trees. The trees are cut down and the wood is turned into pulp, which is made into paper. You can save paper, and trees, by recycling old newspapers to make your own cards and paper.

Paper is rolled into huge sheets, then sold to printers to print newspapers and books.

1 You will need old newspapers, wire mesh, a dishpan, absorbent cloths, a blender, a bucket, thick paper (which you can keep and use again), and water. Tear the newspaper into pieces.

2 Put the pieces in a bucket and cover with water. Soak overnight. Ask an adult to put small amounts of the pulp into the blender and liquefy.

3 Decide on the size of your paper and ask an adult to cut the wire mesh to that size. Pour the liquefied pulp into the dishpan and add water. Stir the mixture. Slide the wire mesh into the mixture.

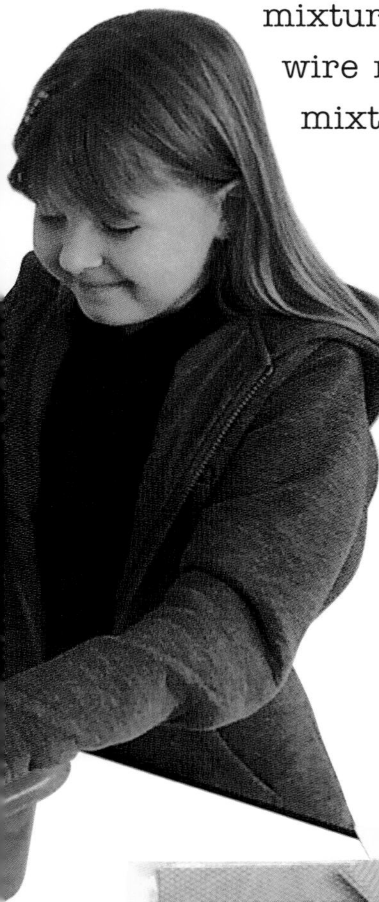

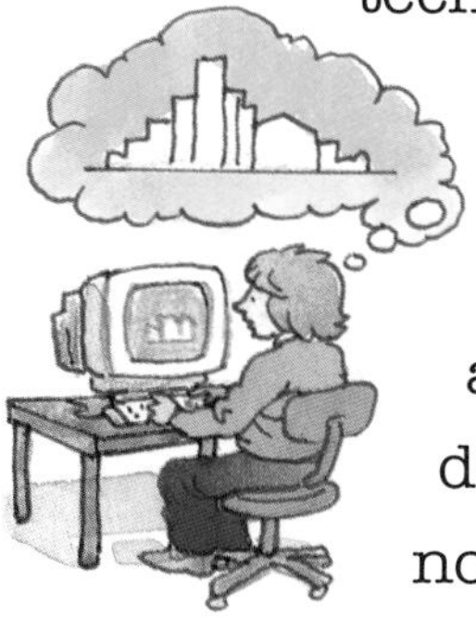

4 Lay a cloth flat on some thick paper. Lift the mesh out of the mixture and lay it on the cloth, pulp side down. Press down on the mesh, then lift it, leaving the layer of pulp on the cloth. Place another cloth, then more thick paper on top of the pulp and press. Repeat these layers, as shown.

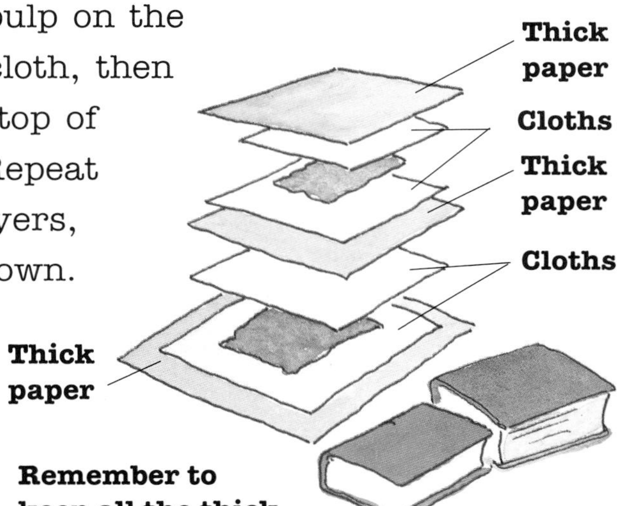

Thick paper

Cloths

Thick paper

Cloths

Thick paper

Remember to keep all the thick paper to use again!

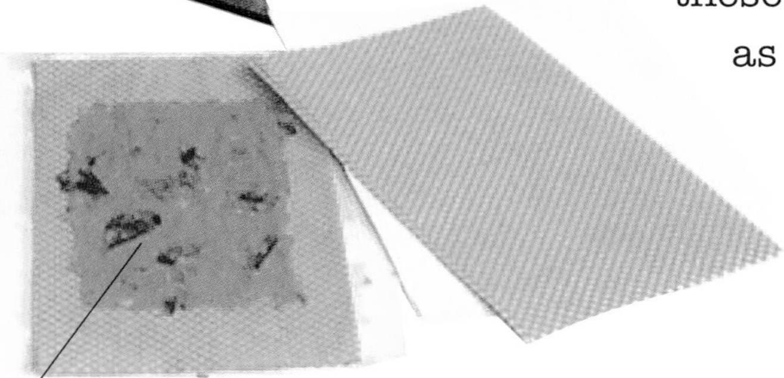

Add colored paper or flowers to the pulp for decoration.

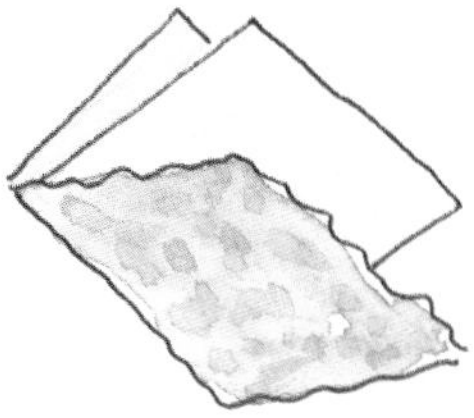

5 Lay some heavy books on top of the last sheet of thick paper. Leave for a few days, then remove the layers. Place your sheets of paper on newspaper to dry. Use your recycled paper to make cards or writing paper.

ENERGY

Most of the energy we use in factories, homes, and cars is created from burning fossil fuels—oil, coal, and natural gas. Fossil fuels cause air pollution when they burn. They give off a gas called carbon dioxide, which gradually builds up in the Earth's atmosphere. Fossil fuels are also nonrenewable, which means they will not last forever. People are looking for other ways to make energy from sources that will not run out, such as the wind, light from the Sun, and running or falling water.

Burning fossil fuels (oil, coal, and gas) releases carbon dioxide gas.

Carbon dioxide builds up in the atmosphere.

Too much carbon dioxide in the atmosphere traps too much heat from the Sun. The Earth gets too warm, making ice melt and sea levels rise. This is called the greenhouse effect.

Burning fossil fuels

WIND POWER

Harness the power of the wind with a windmill. You will need thin paper, a length of dowel, a straight pin, a small bead, scissors, and a ruler.

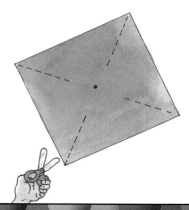

1 Cut out a square from the paper. Mark the center. Draw lines from each corner, almost to the center, as shown here. Cut along the lines.

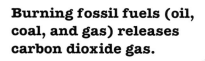

2 Fold each corner into the center, as shown. Fix in place with a pin. Slide the bead onto the pin, behind the windmill.

3 Push the pin into the dowel, with the bead between the windmill and the dowel. Make sure the point of the pin does not stick out. Now stand in the wind and watch your windmill spin around as it captures the energy of the wind.

SOLAR POWER

● Solar energy comes directly from the Sun. Solar power stations (below) or solar panels attached to homes can capture energy from the Sun to provide heat and hot water. In hot deserts it is easy to catch the Sun's energy. It is more difficult in temperate countries that have lots of cloud and rain.

Solar panels

WIND POWER

● Wind turbines are set up in exposed places. The blades may spin through an area more than 200 feet across. The wind turns the turbine blades just as it spins your windmill. The turbines are connected to generators, which produce electricity. Wind energy is renewable and clean, but some say the turbines spoil the scenery.

COUNTRY PROFILE—KENYA

A country is a specific area of land, defined by humans, that is controlled by a single government. There are about 200 countries in the world. Studying a country helps you see how different parts of geography fit together—how places and people affect each other. Kenya is a country in the continent of Africa. Its capital city is Nairobi. The zero degree (0°) line of latitude runs through Kenya, which means it is right on the equator, the hottest part of the world.

PROJECT KENYA

Make a travel poster about Kenya and its people. You will need colored pencils, an atlas, and a large sheet of paper. First, look at a globe or an atlas to locate Africa.

1 Write a list of the things that you need to find out about the country. What kind of climate does Kenya have? Does it have seasons? Are there any mountains? How high are they? Is there a coastline? Use the atlas, go to the library, or use the internet to find the information you need.

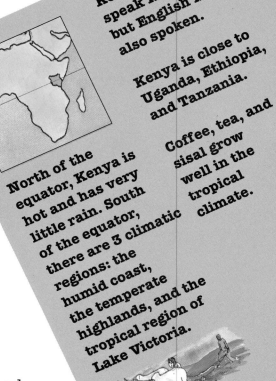

Kenyans mostly speak Kiswahili, but English is also spoken.

Kenya is close to Uganda, Ethiopia, and Tanzania.

North of the equator, Kenya is hot and has very little rain. South of the equator, there are 3 climatic regions: the humid coast, the temperate highlands, and the tropical region of Lake Victoria.

Coffee, tea, and sisal grow well in the tropical climate.

The rainy seasons are: October—December and April—June.

Mount Kenya is part of a chain of volcanic ridges.

TOURISM

● Tourism is one of Kenya's biggest industries. Hundreds of thousands of people visit every year and tourist activities provide jobs for thousands of local people. Many people come to visit the beautiful coastline, but most come to go on safari in one of the country's many national parks, such as Amboseli and the Masai Mara Game Reserve. The national parks are home to wild animals, such as lions, zebras, and elephants.

Kenyan national flag

The Kenyan flag is black, red, and green, with a shield and crossed spears logo in the center.

People eat ugali, a porridge made from cornmeal and water. They also eat irio, made from mashed corn, potatoes, beans, and peas.

In cities, Kenyans live in modern houses or apartments with plumbing and electricity. Farmhouses may be built from logs, branches, and mud. In Nairobi, houses are built from bricks.

2 There are many different tribal groups in Kenya, but most people are Kikuyu. Do some research to find out more about the Kenyan people. What languages do they speak? What kinds of houses do they live in? What are the main industries? What crops are grown? What do people eat? On your large sheet of paper, draw pictures and write labels for all the things you have found out about Kenya and its people.

LANDMARKS

Tourists visit landmarks all over the world. Some are specially built by humans, as monuments to a great event or person. The Taj Mahal in India was built by Shah Jehan in the seventeenth century as a tomb for his wife. Others are historic buildings or structures—such as Tower Bridge in London—which are famous for their design or for something that happened there in the past. Many landmarks are natural wonders, like waterfalls or mountains. Postcards often show landmarks.

Uluru, or Ayer's Rock, Australia

Taj Mahal, Agra, India

Tower Bridge, London, England

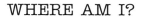

WHERE AM I?

Learn about landmarks in this game. You will need small pictures of different landmarks, cardboard, scissors, glue, and an atlas.

1 Collect postcards or cut out pictures from old magazines. Glue them onto pieces of cardboard.

2 Look in the atlas to find the location of every landmark. On the back of each card, write a few clues about the landmark, such as the capital of the country it is in.

3 Two or more players can play. One person is the tourist and holds up each picture in turn, asking "Where am I?" Players must guess the name of the country or city from the picture. Give clues if no one gets it on the first try. Whoever gets the answer keeps the card. The winner is the player who collects the most cards.

CHANGING NAMES

● Names are like labels. But names on maps are often changed. Landmarks, streets, towns, and sometimes whole countries are given new names. Zaire, a country in Africa, was renamed the Democratic Republic of Congo. Czechoslovakia, in Eastern Europe, divided into two countries, the Czech Republic and Slovakia. The city of Constantinople is now Istanbul and Bombay is Mumbai.

● Settlements in different places often have the same name. There is a city called Birmingham in England and another one in Alabama, U.S.A. There is a Boston, England and a Boston, Massachusetts, U.S.A. Names can be clues to the past. Many people who

migrated and settled in other countries named their new homes with familiar names from their home countries.

POPULATION FACTS AND FIGURES

The world's population, now just over 6 billion, is expected to reach approximately 11 billion by the year 2050.

Country populations

China—1.2 billion
India—1 billion
U.S.A.—281 million
Indonesia—209 million
Bangladesh—127 million
Mexico—97 million
France—58.8 million
United Kingdom—
   58.6 million
Colombia—41.5 million
Kenya—29.5 million
Australia—18.7 million
Sweden—8.9 million
Singapore—3.5 million
Botswana—1.5 million

Population density (people per sq km)

Singapore—6,046
Bangladesh—847
India—291
United Kingdom—
   238
France—107
Indonesia—105
Kenya—57
Mexico—49
Colombia—32
U.S.A.—29
China—20
Sweden—18
Botswana—3
Australia—2

People

● One in six people in the world today lives in poverty.

● Today, around 95 percent of babies are born in developing countries, where food and water are often scarce.

● Developed countries consume the bulk of the world's food, fuel, and water and cause the most environmental damage.

● The U.S.A. consumes one hundred times more energy than Bangladesh.

● It takes nature a million years to produce the amount of oil that the United Kingdom uses in one year.

● Denmark makes four percent of its electricity from wind power.

GLOSSARY

altitude
Height above sea level.

climate
The average weather in a place over the year.

deforestation
The clearing of forest.

developed countries
Countries where there are lots of industries and most people have a high standard of living.

developing countries
Countries where there are few industries and many people live in poverty.

equator
An imaginary line around the center of the Earth at zero degrees (0˚) latitude.

fossil fuels
Fuels like coal, oil, and natural gas, formed from the remains of living things.

generation
The period of about 20 years that separates parents and children.

greenhouse effect
The trapping of too much heat inside the Earth's atmosphere, due to high levels of carbon dioxide caused by burning fossil fuels.

hamlet
A small village.

high-tech industries
Modern, scientific industries, such as computer manufacturing.

latitude
Distance in degrees north or south of the equator. Lines of latitude are parallel to the equator.

longitude
Distance in degrees east or west of the prime meridian.

metropolitan area
Towns and cities joined into one big urban area.

mineral
Any nonliving matter. Rocks and metals are made up of minerals.

pedestrian
A person who walks in an urban area.

population density
The average number of people living in each square kilometer or other unit of area.

prime meridian
An imaginary line that circles the Earth north to south at 0˚ longitude.

refugee
A person seeking shelter from danger by moving to another country.

rural
Located in the country.

settlement
A place where people live.

shanty town
A poor area of a city where homes are made from discarded materials.

urban
Located in a town or city.

INDEX

PICTURE CREDITS
Abbreviations: t-top, m-middle, b-bottom, r-right, l-left, c-center.
All photographs supplied by Select Pictures, except for:
4ml, 28 all, 30b—Digital Stock. 14ml, 14mr, 14bl—E&D Hosking/FLPA
-Images of Nature. 14c—Derek Hall/FLPA-Images of Nature. 15br —
Terry Whittaker/FLPA-Images of Nature. 22c—Philip Gould/CORBIS.